Helen McGinn is the author of the award-winning wine blog and book, *The Knackered Mother's Wine Club*. She spent almost a decade sourcing wines around the world as a supermarket wine buyer and spent the next half-decade pregnant. She now writes about drinks for the *Daily Mail* and *Waitrose Food* magazine and regularly appears as a TV wine expert on BBC1's *Saturday Kitchen* and ITV's *This Morning*. Awards for her blog include Fortnum & Mason's Online Drinks Writer and *Red* magazine's Best Blogger. She is also a bestselling fiction author. Helen is married with three children and lives in the New Forest, and she's hopeless with a hangover.

Twitter: @knackeredmutha
Instagram: @knackeredmother
Facebook: knackeredmotherswineclub
Website: www.knackeredmotherswineclub.com

Also by Helen McGinn

Homemade Cocktails

A Wine Expert's Guide to the Best Booze-Free Drinks

....

ROBINSON

ROBINSON

First published in Great Britain in 2016 by Robinson as *Helen McGinn's Teetotal Tipples, for January and Beyond*

This revised and updated edition published in 2022 by Robinson

10 9 8 7 6 5 4 3 2

Copyright © Helen McGinn, 2016, 2022

The moral right of the author has been asserted.

Important Note
The recommendations in this book are solely intended as education and information and should not be taken as medical advice. All prices are UK and correct at the time of going to press.

A CIP catalogue record for this book is available from the British Library.

ISBN: 978-1-47214-729-5

Typeset in Sentinel Light by Hewer Text UK Ltd, Edinburgh
Printed and bound in Great Britain by Clays Ltd, Elcograf S.p.A.

Papers used by Robinson are from well-managed forests and other responsible sources.

Robinson
An imprint of
Little, Brown Book Group
Carmelite House
50 Victoria Embankment
London EC4Y 0DZ

An Hachette UK Company
www.hachette.co.uk

www.littlebrown.co.uk

Contents

Introduction

OK, first things first. I never, ever thought I'd be writing a book about not drinking. For a start, I spent almost a decade as a supermarket wine buyer, scouring vineyards across the world and sniffing out the good stuff. And for the last ten years I've devoted my working hours to tasting, talking and writing about it, not to mention my non-working hours simply enjoying the stuff. Wine courses through my veins, literally. I love the fact that it usually comes with a brilliant story – who made it, how, where and why – and that with so many to try, I'm properly spoilt for choice. Booze is such a big part of my life I couldn't imagine a world without it. Well, I could, but it wouldn't be as interesting, or nearly as much fun. Sipping a condensation-on-glass cold and very delicious white while catching up on news with a friend or savouring a big glass of red over dinner is, for me, one of life's real pleasures. And as the greeting card goes, no love story ever started with two people sharing a salad.

But then something unexpected happened. I did my first 'dry' January in 2016. Not voluntarily, you understand. The very idea of it always struck me as a rather bad one, encouraging an all-or-nothing approach when actually, for alcohol, (mostly) little and often is my preferred route. And I didn't do it for the obvious reason – health – although let's talk more about that for a moment. As much as we might do a little fist pump whenever we read a report that says drinking red wine is good for you, we know that drinking too much is definitely not a good idea. Just as eating too many bacon butties is not a good idea. Anyway, current government guidelines suggest that we don't drink any more than fourteen units a week for both men and women. That's seven to ten glasses of wine, depending on the size of the glass and the strength of what's in it. Now, I know my limits. And I know that as I've gotten older, I can't drink as much as I used to. In fact, I simply don't want to drink as much as I used to. I'm drinking less, but better, generally. I also know that even with at least two to three booze-free nights a week throughout the year (I probably won't do a dry January again, life is too short!), I'm usually on the outer limits of those particular limits. Still, overall I drink in moderation (mostly) and for pleasure (always).

Anyway, as I was saying, the reason I did a dry January wasn't really based on health grounds at all, although if ever there was a month to make me feel like I've had more than my fill of booze or chocolate for a while, it's December. Rather, it was because I'd read an article about 'wine face'. Yes, I am *that* shallow. But bear with. It's a condition identified by a skin specialist, Dr Nigma Talib. She cites droopy eyelids, redness and puffy skin around the eyes as a symptom. Wait, there's more: enlarged pores, dehydrated skin and deep nasolabial folds (ew!). Now, I didn't think I looked *that* hangdog but the suggestion that stopping drinking would make my eyelids less droopy? Suddenly it seemed like quite a good idea. More than that, I just wanted to know if it really would make that big a difference to someone like me, who enjoys a glass of wine or two most nights and a little more at the weekends.

I was writing an article about the experience for a newspaper, so to properly understand the effect that not drinking for a month would have on the skin I had my face scanned before and after the dry month. And so it was on New Year's Eve that I raised my glass (of very good Champagne) at midnight, took one very long sip and put my glass down for the last time. The next morning, as others nursed their (far worse) hangovers, I sipped my coffee and felt just a little bit smug. Even when the Bloody Marys hit the table at 12 p.m. on New Year's Day after a long walk – a family tradition – I didn't mind that I was the only one sticking to mineral water. But a few days in, it suddenly hit me just why it was going to be so hard: because one of my favourite things about having a glass of wine is choosing what to have in the first place. Obviously the choice of wines available is bordering on the ridiculous. With so many to pick from it's sometimes completely overwhelming. Even having a G&T is now fraught with decisions. Which gin: juniper-heavy or floral? What tonic to go for, to garnish or not to garnish, it's enough to drive you to . . . you know where this is going.

But when it came to choosing a soft option, it suddenly all felt a bit, well, flat. I was happy drinking water all day long; I've been doing that for long enough. In the evening, however,

I wanted something a little more satisfying. Something that marked a change from the rush and noise of the day to the easier, more relaxed pace of the evening – and another glass of water from the tap wasn't cutting it. What I wanted was a grown-up drink, just without alcohol. Not sugar-loaded canned fizzy drinks (I associate those with emergency hangover situations), and not the sweet, bottled cordials I drank too much of throughout my years of being pregnant. No, what I wanted was a drink with a bit of theatre to it. Something I could make and enjoy the ritual of making, much as I enjoyed the ritual of choosing and opening a bottle of wine or making up the perfect G&T (once all those fraught decisions had been made, of course).

And I wanted to be able to make drinks using stuff I had in the cupboard rather than having to take out a second mortgage to buy special ingredients that I'd probably never use again. And so my search for the best grown-up teetotal tipples began. During that time, I found that grown-up drinks have come a long way in recent years. We've now got more non-alcoholic wines on the shelves than ever before. We've got booze-free beer that actually tastes like beer and we've even got alcohol-free spirits. Problem is, just like the ones with alcohol, quality varies enormously. And you can't always judge a book by its cover, or indeed bottle by its label.

What you'll find in this book is a collection of easy-to-make booze-free drinks, along with my pick of the best-tasting ready-to-drink drinks and non-alcoholic beers, wines and spirits around. I've tasted my way through hundreds of bottles and flavour combinations to get here and all have been picked because they feel and taste like a great alternative to alcohol.

What you won't find is any smoothie talking. I love a smoothie, but only if it's for breakfast. And besides, my kids love them too, so they don't really count as a somewhat sophisticated alternative to alcohol. Rather, this is about getting through a dry spell with something grown-up and gorgeous in your glass at the end of the day. None of them are a faff to find ingredients for or to make once you've got them. And all are guaranteed to make you feel like you're not missing out.

There are tips on how to get through even the toughest times, when you're the only non-drinker round the table or at the party, as well as what to drink if you're pregnant. Then, once you've done your dry spell, you'll have a list of what to look for when replenishing your wine rack. We'll also take a closer look at the rise of 'healthy' wines, including natural, organic and sugar-free ones.

Whatever your reasons for not drinking, this book will make it more fun than you could ever imagine. So much so, you really won't miss the booze – at least temporarily, anyway.

Wine Face: A Thing?

Before we get to the drinks, here's what did actually happen to my face after a month of not drinking. Not that much in the first few weeks, to be honest. In fact, far from waking up bright-eyed and bushy-tailed, I felt even more knackered than usual. Also, no instant weight loss. Rather, two weeks in and I'd put on a few pounds. But, and it's a *big* but, when I looked at the before and after scans of my face (taken with a machine at a clinic in London) the difference was obvious. The wrinkles around my eyes had reduced and my skin was more hydrated. Overall, it looked brighter, tighter and healthier. My skin was cleaner, less congested and with an improved texture. But that wasn't just because of the lack of booze: the fact that I slept better (no late night loo trips!) and drank a lot more water than usual all helped.

So yes, 'wine face' really is a thing, just as 'lack of sleep face' is a thing. But more than ending up with better skin, what I really enjoyed about my dry spell was that living without wine made me appreciate it even more when it was all over. As I've already mentioned, I've moved to a less-but-better approach to wine as I've gotten older. (Having said that, my G&Ts are definitely a little stiffer nowadays!) Anyway, it's about making what I do drink count. And I think that's just as important when you go booze-free.

Store Cupboard Essentials

Right, if we're going to make grown-up, non-alcoholic drinks interesting, we need some basic ingredients. And we need them to look the part. That means having a suitable glass. Just because we're not drinking wine, doesn't mean we can't use a wine glass. The same goes for your spirit-friendly, heavy glass tumblers. Use your best glasses. And we're not going to hold back on the garnishes, either. Except, maybe, cocktail umbrellas. Unless you really do have some of those in the back of the cupboard, in which case have them on standby – shame to waste them. On the next page there is a list, just so we know exactly what glass I'm referring to when a specific glass is mentioned throughout the book. By the way, I haven't listed a cocktail shaker because all of the mocktails in this book can be knocked up in moments and mixed in the glass. Of course if you want to use one, then do. Just don't expect me to wash it up.

Glasses & Equipment

The **Tumbler*** – a must for mocktails

The **Tall Glass*** – or highball, for when you need lots of ice

The **Wine Glass*** – a clear, tulip-shaped one if possible

The **Champagne Flute*** – great for sham-pagne drinks

The **Martini Glass*** – gloriously decadent to drink from

The **Kilner Glass* (with a handle)** – for hot drinks

A **Small, Sharp Knife** and a **Small Chopping Board** of any kind

A **Blender** or **Food Processor** – or even a **Hand Blender**

A **Tea Strainer** – sometimes we'll need to get the bits out of squashed ingredients

Plastic Straws

A **Glass Jug** – handy if you've got one, at least 1-litre capacity

A **Long Wooden Spoon** – useful; if not, stir with a straw

Muslin and a **Fine Metal Sieve** – it's a good idea to have both to hand for cordials

A **Vegetable Peeler** – for garnishes

A **Wooden Spoon** and a **Small Whisk** – both useful

A **Wooden Rolling Pin**, **Clean Linen Towel** or **Freezer Bags** – for crushing ice

* The glasses I use – wine, Martini and flutes – all hold around 200ml comfortably. Any more and I'd spill it.

Sweet Enough

Many of the drinks in this book have relatively little or no added sugar but some of the mocktails call for a dash of sugar syrup. It's easy enough to make. Simply mix equal parts sugar with warm water and shake together in a jam jar until the sugar has dissolved. Or you can simply buy a bottle (I use Monin pure cane sugar syrup, about £2.25 for a small 25cl bottle from larger supermarkets). Sometimes I've used a dash of agave syrup, usually found lurking in the back of my drinks cupboard but, really, any sugar syrup will do, home-made or shop-bought.

Grenadine is the other syrup that pops up. Drinking anything with grenadine in it makes me feel like I'm on holiday. Originally made from pomegranates, hence the deep red colour, it adds a sweet, tart touch to a cocktail or, in our case, mocktail – along with that brilliant colour, obviously. I use one from the French brand Teisseire, available in most supermarkets (about £4.50 for a 60cl bottle). It does have a truckload of sugar in it, but is only ever added as a dash.

Ice, Ice, Baby

When it comes to making a G&T, I've always gone long on ice, cramming as much into the glass as I possibly could. The theory is that by keeping it cold, it'll stay stronger for longer as the ice won't dilute so quickly. Obviously, we're not talking about alcohol in this case but even though we don't need to worry about strength, we're still concerned with flavour. So unless the recipe states any more than usual, four ice cubes is enough to keep it cold.

Stock up on a bag of ice cubes for the freezer. And keep a few in trays of ice, especially if you want some with interesting shapes or with something frozen inside them such as berries or lavender tips (always good to perk up a glass of fizzy water). And if novelty shapes are your thing (they're definitely mine), you can find pretty much anything you like – flamingoes, fish, you name it. My heart-shaped plastic ice cube tray is a particular favourite.

Just the Tonic

A lot of the recipes call for tonic water as a base. Given that not all tonics are created equal, here's a bit of background. Originally, tonic water was a way of getting British soldiers in the 1820s in far-flung places to imbibe quinine, protecting them against malaria. Found in the bark of the cinchona tree, it was quinine that gave the water its trademark bitter character. Today's tonic waters still contain quinine, albeit in relatively low quantities. And as well as your bog standard no-frills tonic waters, there are now lots of really smart tonic waters to choose from. These contain ingredients like bitter orange and natural sugars, rather than the artificial sweeteners found in many ordinary tonic waters. So, much like choosing a gin got more complicated, so has choosing a tonic. In fact, the smarter (more expensive) tonics are the fastest-growing sector of the entire mixer market.

Now, I love opening a can of tonic, for the sound as much as anything else. Also, it reminds me of every minibar I used to know. Which in turn reminds me of a time, pre-children, when we used to stay in the kind of places that indeed had minibars. Nowadays, I usually have a few cans lurking in my fridge and bottles stashed in the cupboard. Some are plain, others flavoured with exotic ingredients. None of them are slimline because I'd rather have a bit of sugar than a whole lot of artificial sweetener, which can leave a slightly bitter taste in the mouth. For drinks with tonic, I use Fever-Tree.

WATER, WATER, EVERYWHERE

When it comes to drinking water at home, I'd rather drink it from a tap than from a bottle. But if I want a glass of water with bubbles, my fizz of choice is Badoit (about £1 for 1 litre), served in a heavy tumbler with a chunk of ice. With its salty tang, tiny bubbles and slightly softer-than-normal feel, it adds a certain *je ne sais quoi* to having a glass of water.

LIQUID CONVERSIONS

IMPERIAL	METRIC	AMERICAN
½fl oz	15ml	1 tablespoon
1fl oz	30ml	2 tablespoons
2fl oz	60ml	¼ cup
4fl oz	120ml	½ cup
8fl oz	240ml	1 cup
16fl oz	480ml	2 cups

In British, Australian and many Canadian recipes an imperial pint is 20fl oz. American recipes use the American pint measurement, which is 16fl oz.

PART ONE

Mocktails & Infusions

The thing about cocktails is that they're more than just a drink: they are a promise, often marking the start of a far-from-ordinary evening. Once, in a particularly lovely hotel bar not far from where I live, I ordered a Martini as my pre-prandial. It shook the taste buds into action ahead of dinner. It brought a flush to my cheeks and it made me feel... Oh. So. Sophisticated. For a moment, I could pretend I was the kind of woman who always sipped slowly on a Martini before dinner rather than one who had to position her hair over an old unidentified (children's) food stain on a navy silk top to cover it up.

....

Anyway, fact is, cocktails are one of life's perkiest perks but here, we're talking cocktails without the essential ingredient: alcohol. In which case, they'd better be good. Because if we're taking out the ingredient that gives a drink its kick, what's left is at risk of tasting a little hollow. So, to get around that, all of the recipes here rely on ingredients with plenty of flavour and in some cases, colour. And some of them are savoury rather than sweet, which seems to trick the mind (mine, anyway) into thinking the drink is more grown-up and sophisticated. The idea is that these drinks will be something you'll want to sip slowly both before and with food.

Most of them are simple enough to knock up in minutes but a few require a little more faff (anything with a blender counts as a faff, due to extra washing-up). As for measurements, most are given in parts rather than specific amounts so that you can tailor them to whatever format – small bottle or can – your mixer might come in. Basically, there's a booze-less drink to fit your mood whether you just want to chuck a few things in a glass and be done with it or to put something together that deserves a polite round of applause, even if you are on your own.

GINGER & BASIL SPARKLER

There's something about the taste of ginger that feels like it's doing me good. It's refreshing, it's got plenty of flavour and it manages to both cleanse and refresh the palate. Pregnancy saw me craving ginger. I used to eat it raw, in chunks, which I swear helped ease that horrible early pregnancy sickness that just wouldn't go away. Anyway, during my dry month, ginger was definitely one of my saviour flavours. And it's still the one that I go back to most often on my wine-free days.

Handful of ice cubes
200ml ginger ale
Sprig of fresh basil leaves
Slice of fresh lime

Put a handful of ice cubes into a tumbler and fill up with ginger ale. Add a sprig of basil leaves, torn if you want more obvious basil flavours or just as it is if you prefer more of a ginger hit. Add a slice of lime and pop in a straw so you can mix it up from time to time as you sip.

SEEDLIP & TONIC

This drink has got a lot to answer for. I first came across Seedlip (www.seedlipdrinks.com) when a friend asked me if I could get hold of any for her, as she wanted to buy it as a Christmas present for her husband. Due to illness, he was off the booze and she'd read about it somewhere. So I called up the man who made it and asked where I could buy some. 'You can't, it's all gone,' he said. This was Ben Branson, Seedlip's creator. Seeing an opportunity to solve the 'what to drink when you're not drinking' dilemma, Ben created a non-alcoholic distilled spirit using an old copper still and a selection of botanicals including cloves, barks and citrus peels. It's aromatic, savoury and reassuringly bitter. Basically, it's like having a G&T, but with a non-alcoholic 'gin'. His first batch sold out within weeks but, happily, he's somewhat upped his quantities since then as well as creating more styles including one called Garden 108, which is more herbal and leafier in flavour, and the citrusy Grove 42.

The recipe below uses the original Seedlip, Spice 94, which is rather woodier and, well, reassuringly medicinal in character, but you could use any of them. Seedlip is both sugar- and sweetener-free, with no artificial flavours or colourings. And it comes as beautifully packaged as any good boutique gin. Similar in price, too, at around £26 for a standard 70cl bottle. Not cheap, but it really is a brilliantly refreshing idea, not to mention a seriously credible non-alcoholic alternative to a stiff G&T. And because you sip it slowly, one bottle lasts for ages.

Handful of ice cubes
1 part Seedlip Spice 94
2 parts tonic water
Slice of fresh lemon or a twist of lemon peel*

Put a handful of ice cubes into a tumbler or tall glass, depending on what kind of day you've had. Pour in one part Seedlip to two parts tonic water. Serve with either a slice of fresh lemon or just a twist of lemon peel, again depending on what kind of day you've had.

* I favour a generous strip of lemon peel taken off with a vegetable peeler over a thin strip done with a paring knife (pure laziness). Either way, try to get as much of the yellow skin and as little of the white pith as possible. Take the strip and twist it gently with your fingertips – think pig's tail – before popping it into the glass.

POMEGRANATE SPARKLER

On its own I find pomegranate juice a bit too full on, flavour-wise. And some of the brands are just too sweet for me. But add some sparkling mineral water and you get a long pink drink with bright flavours. PomeGreat is a good one; it's not made from concentrate but it does have a fair bit of sugar in it. You can, of course, make your own pomegranate juice but given that I find extracting just a handful of seeds to sprinkle on a salad a bit of a faff, leaving me slightly sweaty and sweary, I'd rather buy ready-made. By the way, pomegranate juice is reputed to increase the sex drive. Just saying . . .

Handful of ice cubes
1 part pomegranate juice
2 parts sparkling mineral water
Slice of fresh lime
Sprig of fresh mint

Chuck a handful of ice into a tumbler. Pour over one part pomegranate juice to two parts sparkling mineral water. Give it a stir with a straw. Add a slice of fresh lime and a sprig of fresh mint to serve. Wink at your other half as you take your first sip.

SIMPLE VIRGIN MARY

As cocktails go, a Bloody Mary is right up there, near the top of my Favourite Cocktails list. And happily for me, my husband makes a bloody good one. We're talking properly spicy, with lots of seasoning and a generous slug of vodka. It's the only cocktail I would ever contemplate drinking before midday (and I'm including Buck's Fizz, a terrible waste of Champagne in my opinion). Not that I often drink cocktails before midday, but there are occasions when only a Bloody Mary will do. I've mentioned New Year's Day already, but when your Sunday needs a pre-lunch kick-start and you've got a house full of people, put a jug of Bloody Mary on the table and suddenly everyone wants one.

The reason a Bloody Mary works as a non-alcoholic drink is that, for a start, it's got plenty of flavour. With tomato juice as the base, you can pep it up with a dash of this and a pinch of that. When going for the virgin version, I keep it simple but you could throw pretty much everything at it – cayenne pepper, mustard powder, horseradish. Talking of fresh horseradish, it's not what I'd call a staple in my house but I've usually got about five jars of horseradish sauce in the cupboard at any one time. Two of them will be open, one of them past its sell-by date and the others are duplicates because it's one of those things I always buy because I always think we've run out. Anyway, in the absence of freshly grated horseradish, my husband adds a dash of horseradish sauce to his mix but I prefer it without. As for the rest, chuck in whatever you can find from the list below but don't worry too much if you're an ingredient down: improvise and try a touch of something else.

For the tomato juice, I love The Tomato Stall's pure tomato juice made from Isle of Wight tomatoes (£2.50 for 500ml or £1.95 for 250ml, www.thetomatostall.co.uk). Then I can spice it up according to taste. A really quick fix is pre-spiced tomato juice, like Big Tom (widely available, approximately £2.85 for 750ml). It's made from concentrate but has a good, earthy taste with plenty of punchy spice to it. You could, if you're feeling really keen, make your own tomato juice by blanching four fresh tomatoes in hot water, peeling and de-seeding them and then blitzing them in a blender, but given that I like mine spicy, and more importantly I'm too lazy to do it myself, fresh juice from a bottle or carton does the job. Spice it up or tone it down as you please.

Handful of ice cubes
200ml tomato juice
Black pepper to taste
Pinch of celery salt (or salt flakes)
Squeeze of fresh lemon juice
Dash of Worcestershire sauce
Few drops of Tabasco
Freshly grated horseradish or a scant ¼ tsp from a jar
   (optional)
Slice of fresh lemon and a celery stick (optional) to
   garnish

Take a tall glass and fill with ice, then pour over as much tomato juice as you like. Add a touch of black pepper, a pinch of celery salt (or salt flakes), a squeeze of fresh lemon juice, a dash of Worcestershire sauce, a few drops of Tabasco to taste and the horseradish, if using. Stir it around with a long spoon – or the celery stick.

Alternatively, chuck all the ingredients in a blender (except the ice cubs – just add those in after) and give it a really quick blitz before pouring it into a glass. Add a slice of fresh lemon. The celery stick garnish is optional (I happen to think (a) instant canapé and (b) you can stir your Virgin Mary with it).

COFFEE TONIC

Soho legend has it that a supermodel once walked into a bar and asked for a drink that would 'Wake me up then f*ck me up'. And so the Espresso Martini was born and the rest, as they say, is slightly hazy. Anyway, a non-alcoholic solution for a caffeine kick with a difference is a coffee tonic. Suddenly these are everywhere. You can make them with cold coffee but I like them made with a hot shot of espresso (also, I'm too impatient to wait for my drink to cool down). It's a bit bizarre on first taste but the balance of bitterness and freshness is fabulous. It'll wake you up, for sure.

1 shot hot espresso
Handful of ice cubes
200ml tonic water

First, get your shot of espresso on the go. While it's brewing, fill a tall glass with a handful of ice cubes. Pour in the tonic water and once the coffee is ready, pour it over the top and give it a stir with a long spoon. Sip on the coffee foam at the top before it disappears.

ELDERFLOWER FIZZ

After almost five years of being permanently pregnant, it took me a while to fall back in love with elderflower cordial. Back then it was as if this was the *only* non-alcoholic drink available on the planet, other than water. Thing is, my fussy pregnant taste buds made it taste metallic and horrible. I developed a real aversion to the stuff and honestly, it took me years to love it again. But now, served properly (i.e. with lots of ice in a beautiful glass, cold to the touch), it's one of my favourite non-drink drinks. You could add sparkling mineral water but I love the combination of the sweetness of the elderflower with the grown-up bitterness of the tonic water.

Handful of ice cubes
1 part elderflower cordial (bought or homemade, see
    page 12), chilled
4 parts tonic water, chilled
Slice of fresh lemon

Fill a tall glass with a handful of ice cubes. Add one part elderflower cordial to four parts tonic water. Both cordial and tonic should be fridge-cold. Add a slice of lemon to serve.

HOMEMADE ELDERFLOWER CORDIAL

Makes 1.5 litres, which I split between two Kilner clip-top bottles, each with a 1-litre capacity

If it gets to that time of year when the hedgerows bloom with elderflowers (May and June is the time to be on the lookout in the UK) and you decide you are going to make your own elderflower cordial, there are tons of recipes around – all with different steeping times, amounts of sugar and added ingredients. My favourite is this one, with a whopping four-day steeping time. It gives the resulting cordial a gorgeous proper hedgerow character, which goes some small way to making up for the lack of alcohol. There's also something pleasingly therapeutic about inhaling the (increasingly floral) scent each day as you lift the tea towel covering the pot to give it a stir.

    20 whole elderflower heads, no stalks (gathered just
        as the buds are opening)
    1.5 litres water
    1kg sugar
    Juice and zest of 3 fresh lemons
    Juice and zest of 1 fresh orange
    1 tsp citric acid (optional)

Gently rinse the elderflower heads and drain on kitchen paper or blow on them to get rid of any lurking insects. Pour the water into a large pan, add the sugar and bring to the boil.

Turn off the heat and add the elderflower heads together with the juice and zest of the lemons and orange. Add the citric acid, if using (I do: it makes it less cloudy). Cover and leave in a cool place for four days, stirring once daily, then pour it through a muslin-lined sieve (to catch any little bugs) into a jug before pouring into sterilised bottles.

To sterilise the bottles, I just put them through a quick dish-washer cycle. But you can also soak them in hot soapy water, rinse and leave to dry in a very low oven (100°C/225°F/Gas 4).

The cordial will keep in the fridge for about four weeks, although mine barely lasts two weeks because the children go through it at an alarming rate.

PINK LEMONADE

As much as I love a simple Citron Pressé – fresh lemon juice, sugar and cold water mixed to taste – it's best served in a big jug on a hot day. So this Pink Lemonade is my way of perking up the evening with something I can throw together in no time, even if it is just for one. Obviously the grenadine adds some sweetness, so we can leave out the sugar here. I mean, it's practically a health drink!

Handful of ice cubes
Sparkling mineral water
Juice of half a fresh lemon
Dash of grenadine

Put a handful of ice cubes into a tall glass and fill it two-thirds full with sparkling mineral water. Add the juice of half a lemon and a dash of grenadine until it's as pink as you want it. Stir with a straw and serve.

If making up quantities for more than one, I usually make up a litre at a time as this is what fits in my favourite jug.

CUCUMBER WATER

Makes approximately 1 litre

I'm not exactly sure when I started noticing slivers of cucumber peel in the water at restaurants but suddenly, no water carafe was complete without it. It's such a simple idea but so effective and delicious, especially on a hot day. But when it gets to the evening, adding a slice or sliver of cucumber to a glass of sparkling water feels a bit half-hearted so to zhuzh it up a bit, we're adding some other bits and pieces. I make this in my favourite carafe with stacking tumblers.

This is inspired by my brilliant friends Lucy and Claire McDonald, authors of the fantastic *Crumbs* book; I love their salty take on it.

  1.5-litre bottle of sparkling mineral water (enough left
      over to top up or drink up the next day)
  Dash of fresh lemon or lime juice
  Sprig of fresh mint
  Pinch of sea salt flakes or a dash of sugar syrup
  Lots of ice cubes
  ½–1 cucumber*

This works best if made up in a glass jug. Pour in a bottle of sparkling mineral water and add a dash of lemon or lime juice (or both if you're feeling really reckless). Stick in a sprig of mint and add a pinch of sea salt if you want it savoury. If you're in the mood for sweeter rather than savoury, substitute the salt for a dash of sugar syrup (a teaspoonful works for me). Add lots of ice cubes and stir in the cucumber. Add the whole lot if you want it really cucumber-y, or just half if you prefer it simply cucumber-kissed.

* You can either add take slivers off with a vegetable peeler or just chop it into chunks. Thinly sliced will give it more flavour (and looks rather more lovely).

MOSC-NO MULE

Some of my most memorable (and I use that term fairly loosely here) evenings have been kick-started with a Moscow Mule. I absolutely love them, especially when served in the traditional copper mug that seems to have become the only acceptable vessel from which to sip this American creation. The combination of ginger beer, lime juice and vodka gives it such a whack of flavour. Happily, the double whammy of lime and ginger makes it one of the best cocktails to mock. It manages to cope without the vodka just fine, as long as everything else is kick-ass. Here's a recipe for one, but you can always crank up the quantities and make a jug of it if everyone else wants one (which they will, once they see your cool copper mug).

   Handful of ice cubes
   200ml ginger beer (Fever-Tree single-serve bottles
      are 200ml)
   Dash of sugar syrup
   Juice of ½–1 fresh lime
   Sprig of fresh mint

Fill your copper mug or tumbler with a handful of ice cubes. Pour over the ginger beer then add a dash of sugar syrup and the juice of half a lime or a whole one if you wish (I tend to use half and save the other half for another drink later in the week). Stick in a sprig of mint on the side and give it a stir with a straw.

NO-JITO

The great thing about this being a No-Jito rather than a Mojito is we don't have to argue about which is the best rum to use (although, for the record, Havana Club 3 is the answer). Anyway, this cool Cuban refresher is so simple to make and tastes amazing with or without the rum. The key green ingredients – fresh mint and lime – lift the spirits enough. You could add a tablespoon of caster sugar in place of the syrup, but adding a dash of syrup is a doddle and you don't need to dissolve it.

Although it's a bit of a faff, take a minute to crush the ice for this one. Bung a couple of handfuls of ice cubes into a freezer bag or wrap them in a tea towel and whack it about ten times with a rolling pin. Trust me, this is as effective after a bad day as any stiff drink. And I suggest using a good-quality soda water here rather than normal sparkling water – it balances all the flavours better.

About 10 ice cubes
1 fresh lime
Handful of small fresh mint leaves
Dash of sugar syrup
150ml soda water

Put about ten ice cubes into a freezer bag or wrap in a tea towel and crush as described above. Transfer the crushed ice to a tall glass and add the juice of half a lime (about a tablespoon). Add a handful of small mint leaves, preferably the tops of about four sprigs that you've gently squashed in your hand to release the flavour before popping them in. Add a generous dash of sugar syrup (about a teaspoonful suits me) and top with soda water. Stir with a spoon before adding a slice of lime from the half you have left over. Put on some Cuban music and the night is yours.

FELLINI

Once, on holiday in Venice, I had two Bellinis in Harry's Bar. It cost almost as much as our flights to Venice and the glasses were so small, three sips and it was gone. However, it was a simple little drink and utterly delicious, a magical mix of white peach purée and Prosecco – which actually makes it quite a difficult one to turn into a homemade alcohol-free version. Sparkling grape juice is way too sweet, sparkling water too neutral. Making it with a fresh white peach and whizzing it up in the blender doesn't make it any better (and the effort to juice ratio is ridiculous). But then I had one at Lime Wood, a gorgeous hotel down the road from me, made by their bartender. 'It's a perfect fake Bellini!' I cried. 'It's a Fellini,' he replied.

He used white peach purée from Funkin (about £9.30 for a 1kg pack, widely available), topped up with half soda, half lemonade. This gave it the sweetness it needed, along with more bubbly bubbles (technical term, obviously). Then he added a tiny dash of sugar syrup and, to garnish, a sprig of rosemary. And because he's an excellent bartender, it was served in a chilled glass flute. So, extra points to you if you're organised enough to do that at home.

Sprig of fresh rosemary
1 part white peach purée
1 part soda water
1 part lemonade
Dash of sugar syrup

Take a glass flute (chilled if you're on it*) and place a sprig of rosemary inside. Fill with one part white peach purée, one part soda water and one part lemonade (pour slowly and carefully so that you don't burst all the bubbles too quickly). Add a tiny dash of sugar syrup to taste and stir carefully with the rosemary sprig.

Sip slowly, close your eyes and pretend you're in Harry's Bar. And brilliantly, it's not cost you the price of a small car.

* Chill for 10 minutes in the freezer or 20 minutes in the fridge. Alternatively, fill the flute with ice and water and leave for 5 minutes, then tip it out and use immediately.

ALMOST 75

This is one of many, many drinks to appear fleetingly in the film *Casablanca*. And my favourite French 75 cocktail recipe, taken from the must-have *Savoy Cocktail Book* by Harry Craddock, originally published in 1930, brings together Champagne and gin. It's quite the party, as you can imagine. But this is one way to get your kicks without the alcohol. Maybe not a full 75, but the lemony bitterness is so delicious it'll leave you feeling less bitter about not drinking.

½–1 fresh lemon
Dash of sugar syrup
200ml bitter lemon

As with the Fellini (see page 21), use a chilled glass if you can. Add the juice of half a lemon (or a whole one if you want it extra-lemony) and a dash of sugar syrup. Then top up the glass with fridge-cold bitter lemon.

Serve immediately and resist the urge to quote loudly from the film about gin joints.

LIGHT SEA BREEZE

This is a tart little number, thanks to the combination of cranberry and grapefruit juice. And given that vodka doesn't really taste of anything – excluding the flavoured stuff – we're just missing the kick of alcohol here. So, to make up for it, I add a sprinkle of edible glitter (available from most larger supermarkets). Yes, I know that's ridiculously kitsch but we're talking about a *bright pink drink*. Better to embrace it and go all out. If this doesn't brighten up your evening, then I don't know what will.

Handful of ice cubes
1 part grapefruit juice
2 parts cranberry juice
Wedge of fresh lime and a sprinkling of edible glitter
  to garnish

Put a handful of ice cubes into a tumbler. Pour over one part grapefruit juice to two parts cranberry juice and pop a wedge of lime in the top. Then rescue that long-forgotten pot of edible glitter from the back of the cupboard and sprinkle a pinch over the top of the glass. Finally, stir with a straw.

SHIRLEY

A few years ago I went through a phase of pimping my Prosecco with different ingredients. I've tried all sorts: rose syrup (like drinking perfume), a dash of Campari (still my favourite), gin, vodka, bitters (not all at once, obviously). I tried it with a dash of grenadine syrup to get that beautiful pink-at-the-bottom effect, but mixed with the already sweet-ish Prosecco, it was too cloying. But the grenadine came good again when added to ginger ale.

If you were to add fresh orange juice and a maraschino cherry, you'd have a Shirley Temple, the non-alcoholic drink allegedly served to the child star at her tenth birthday party. But I just add a thick slice of orange and plenty of ice so that it's not too sweet and you still get the hit of ginger and the brilliant pink colour that grenadine brings to the non-alcoholic party. No naughty curls with this one!

Handful of ice cubes
200ml ginger ale
Dash of grenadine
Thick slice of fresh orange

Fill a tumbler with a handful of ice cubes. Top up with ginger ale, add a dash of grenadine (it is really sweet so a small rather than a generous dash works for me) and finally pop a thick slice of orange cut in half in the top.

COS-NO

Served in a Martini glass, the alcoholic version has vodka and orange-flavoured liqueur. But the non-alcoholic one is all about citrus fruits – lemon, lime, orange – along with cranberry juice. This is lovely as a short, sharp drink to sip on before supper – and do as Carrie Bradshaw would: drink it from a Martini glass.

Ice cubes
1 fresh orange
Juice of 1 fresh lime
Juice of 1 small fresh lemon
About 30ml cranberry juice

Fill a Martini glass with ice cubes and put it in the fridge. Meanwhile, squeeze the juice of half an orange, one lime and one small lemon into a small jug. Pour in approximately 30ml of cranberry juice (the mixture should be roughly equal parts of the four ingredients) and mix together. Remove the ice and pour the Cos-No into the chilled glass (pour it through a metal sieve or tea strainer if you don't want any bits). Serve garnished with a twist of orange peel (see page 5) for full effect.

FRESH LIME SODA

One of my all-time favourite non-alcoholic drinks, a simple lime soda is a doddle to make and delicious to drink. But to make it a touch more interesting, this one has a dash of both salt and sugar so you get a hit of salty sweetness along with plenty of fresh lime and bubbles. You could make this with lime cordial but I'd rather save my Rose's for a gin gimlet when I'm decidedly not dry. I don't use ice but you can add some if you wish.

    200ml sparkling mineral water
    ½–1 fresh lime (reserve a small wedge to garnish)
    Pinch of salt flakes
    Dash of sugar syrup

Pour the sparkling mineral water into a glass. Add the juice of one lime (or half if you don't want it quite so limey). Add a pinch of salt flakes and a dash of sugar syrup. Bung in a little wedge of lime to make it look lovely and you're done.

WATERMELON & COCONUT SURPRISE

This came about because I bought a watermelon. Obviously I couldn't resist walking into the kitchen and announcing to my husband that I carried a watermelon. Anyway, I bought it for the kids and it was enormous. After three days of watermelon for pudding, they were begging to go back to yoghurts. So there it sat, the other half of the watermelon, taking up over half a shelf in the already-crowded fridge. On the shelf above was a carton of coconut water, bought on offer in the supermarket the previous week. I'd read that it was good for you, would give me shiny hair and solve any bowel problems (*not* that I had any but still nice to know). But when I tried to drink a small glass of it, I simply couldn't – it was *awful*!

I know coconut water has its fans (oh hi, Madonna), but I'm not one of them. So, I still had an almost-full carton of coconut water and half a watermelon. A quick Google search and I'd found a whole heap of recipes, except they usually went by a rather more exotic name like Watermelon Coconut Agua Fresca. I'm sticking with Watermelon & Coconut Surprise because it really did make me see that coconut water wasn't so bad after all. And I wasn't expecting that.

150ml fridge-cold watermelon juice (about 3 big
    hunks of watermelon, see method)
50ml coconut water
Squeeze of fresh lime juice

Handful of ice cubes

Cocktail umbrella to garnish (optional)

Blitz about three big hunks of watermelon in a blender, chill and then pour the juice through a metal sieve into a jug. Pour 50ml of coconut water into a tall glass and add roughly one to three parts watermelon juice, along with a squeeze of lime and a handful of ice cubes.

If you've got any little cocktail umbrellas lurking at the back of the kitchen drawer, now's the time to use one!

WARM APPLE PUNCH

Serves 6

I first made this years ago for a bonfire party (my middle son's birthday is 5 November) and most of my friends were either pregnant or breastfeeding at the time. So I had two pans on the go, one full of mulled wine with an added glug or three of ruby port. The other had this non-alcoholic alternative, a simple apple punch pepped up with some of the same ingredients used in the mulled wine. It went down faster than a windfall apple.

I've listed the ingredients you'll need if making up a batch, given that this recipe is a bit more laborious than most. It'll make six servings but if you want to make up just the one, scale down the quantities accordingly. It's a great one for when the weather's cold or you're just feeling a bit under it – think of it as a hug in a glass.

1 litre apple juice
1 cinnamon stick (plus more for the garnish)
6 cloves
4 wide strips of orange peel
1 knob of stem ginger in syrup, sliced, plus 1 tbsp of the
    syrup
Small pinch of ground allspice

Put all of the ingredients in a saucepan and bring to a simmer, stirring occasionally. Turn the heat down and leave for about

15 minutes, then strain through a sieve into a heatproof jug or straight into Kilner glass mugs. Garnish each one with a cinnamon stick if you don't mind using up a whole jar of them in one go.

SPICED CHAI LATTE

I'm not a great herbal tea drinker. I mean, I love the odd peppermint tea or soothing camomile every now and again. But I think that (a) my love of English Breakfast and Earl Grey and (b) the copious amounts of raspberry leaf tea I had to consume to bring on three late pregnancies (reader, it didn't work) have left me lukewarm for the herbal stuff. But this is another way of doing tea that's both refreshing and comforting at the same time. This is for when your evening involves a sofa, a lot of telly and not much else.

I was a late convert to chai tea. Probably because the first one I ever tried, from a big chain coffee shop, was hideously sweet and expensive to boot. So I played around with a basic recipe, pared it down so that it was store-cupboard simple and adjusted it to get the right balance of flavours to suit me. The warming spices and soothing milk all wrapped up in gentle tea flavours and tannins work beautifully together. And if I can't get my tannin fix from red wine, I'll get it from a cup of tea instead. You might prefer a bit more spice, in which case just dial it up accordingly.

150ml semi-skimmed milk (or almond milk if you
   prefer)
50ml water
¼ tsp ground ginger
¼ tsp ground cloves
¼ tsp ground cinnamon

1 teabag (or ½ tsp loose black tea leaves) – normal
   English Breakfast
Dash of sweetener to taste (agave syrup, maple syrup
   or sugar)

Put all the ingredients except for your sweetener into a saucepan and bring to a gentle simmer. Leave to heat gently for 10 minutes, stirring with a wooden spoon or small whisk every now and again. Once done, leave off the heat for a couple of minutes before pouring through a sieve into a mug or cup. Add a dash of sweetener to taste – I use a teaspoon of agave syrup.

Take it to the sofa, grabbing a blanket on the way.

PART TWO

Non-Alcoholic Wines, Beers & Ciders

*The thing about non-alcoholic wines, beers
and ciders is that they're not, strictly speaking,
non-alcoholic. Most wines, beers and ciders sold
as 'alcohol free' do contain a small percentage of
alcohol, up to 0.05 per cent alcohol by volume to be
precise. De-alcoholised drinks will contain up to
0.5 per cent. The definition of low-alcohol drinks
is anything between 0.5 and 1.2 per cent. For the
purposes of staying dry, I think anything over 1 per
cent feels like cheating. So all the drinks you'll find
mentioned here are less than that.*

....

Most of us want to go low at some point or another, even if
it's just because we're driving. But sometimes you don't want
to take the soft drink option. What you might prefer is something that looks, tastes and feels like wine or beer, just without the alcohol; something that allows you to pour from a
wine bottle or drink from a beer bottle. The real problem has
been finding drinks that do indeed taste anything like their
alcoholic relations, because when you remove the alcohol,
you can lose flavour and aroma, not to mention body. For
years, anything with reduced alcohol had a fairly ropey

reputation, quality-wise. The beers were watery and the wines tasted more like weak fruit squash. Hologram drinks, really: they looked the part but tasted hollow. Happily, the relatively recent development of spinning cone technology, which removes alcohol with less evaporation compared to more traditional techniques, has been a game-changer when it comes to low-alcohol wines.

There aren't many that made it into this chapter, because much of what's on offer just isn't wine-y or beer-y enough. Often they're too sweet, lack natural flavour and feel just a little, well, lightweight. But this selection of alcohol-free and low-alcohol drinks tastes pretty much like the real thing, with the exception of that unmistakable alcoholic hug.

BELLE & CO 0% SPARKLING
AROUND £4 WIDELY AVAILABLE

There are lots of sparkling non-alcoholic 'wines' around but most of them taste more like fizzy grape juice than wine. This one, however, cleverly blends sparkling fermented grape juice with green tea, the latter adding some tannins to the mix. It's fresh, fruity and perfectly drinkable.

LA GIOIOSA
0.0 PER CENT, £6 OCADO

From one of the biggest players on the prosecco scene, this sparkling Italian white is made from the same grape behind prosecco – Glera – but without the alcohol. It's a little drier than most on the palate (often sugar is added to make up for the missing alcohol in many no & low drinks). Suitable for vegans, too.

SAINSBURY'S WINEMAKERS SELECTION ALCOHOL-FREE SPARKLING WINE

0.05 PER CENT, £2.75

www.sainsburys.co.uk

This is an aromatised sparkling wine so it's got added flavourings – in this case grape must (basically, grape juice). Made in Germany from a blend of grapes, it's frothy and fresh, with some good green apple and ripe pear flavours. I've tasted worse Prosecco, to be honest. And you can pimp this for even better results: a quick squeeze of fresh lime adds a proper citrus kick. There's an alcohol-free rosé and red wine in the same range but this is the pick of the bunch.

FIZZERO
0 PER CENT, AROUND £4 M&S

If you want a glass of non-alcoholic pink bubbles, this'll do nicely. It looks the part – great bottle, popping cork, nice enough label – all those boxes are ticked. But most importantly, it tastes pretty good. This, too, is made from a blend of sparkling fermented grape juice blended with green tea (for that extra added mouthfeel), along with strawberry and raspberry notes. Just the thing when you've got to raise a toast, just without the alcohol.

TORRES NATUREO MUSCAT DE-ALCOHOLISED WINE
0.0 PER CENT, £6 WIDELY AVAILABLE

Torres is a big name in Spain, making wine for well over a hundred years. This is their first de-alcoholised wine and, apparently, Spain's first too. What makes it much better than so many others is that it's made from the aromatic Muscat grape, so it's got lots going for it even when the alcohol is removed because it smells grapey, like wine. Not all wines, obviously, but light, fresh, floral ones. With simple pear fruit flavours, this can also work with food: anything herby, fresh and light.

EISBERG ALCOHOL-FREE SAUVIGNON BLANC NV
0.05 PER CENT, £3.50 WIDELY AVAILABLE

I *know!* Eisberg! This alcohol-free wine brand has been around for years and years. And until fairly recently, had the whole alcohol-free shelf to itself in shops. Not that it was really a shelf, more like a spot in the bottom left-hand corner. But the brand has had something of a makeover in recent years and one of the best things to happen is the launch of different grape varieties.

There is a whiff of gooseberry, the classic Sauvignon Blanc tell, but more tropical fruit aromas overall. And, brilliantly, it is fresh, light and not at all sweet. So many alcohol-free drinks use sugar as a way of making up for lost flavour and alcohol that they end up not really tasting like wine at all. Drink it well chilled – and if you're in the mood for a spritzer (don't diss the spritzer, I love a spritzer), go two parts wine to one part soda with plenty of ice and a slice of lemon or lime.

TORRES NATUREO ROSÉ
BOOZE-FREE WINE
0.5 PER CENT, £5.99 WIDELY AVAILABLE

Non-alcoholic rosé offerings are a little thin on the ground. Actually, they're a little thin in the glass, mostly. Torres has made a definitely drinkable one, though, from a blend of Syrah and Cabernet Sauvignon grapes. It tastes a bit like melted boiled sweets but there's a nice whiff of redcurrant fruit to it, together with some decent acidity to hold it together. You can spritz it up by mixing it with one part soda or sparkling mineral water to two parts wine for long drink. Lots of ice is essential.

EISBERG ALCOHOL-FREE ROSÉ
0.05 PER CENT, £3.50 WIDELY AVAILABLE

This one's light and fresh with barely-but-there red fruit aromas, which is what you want with a rosé, with or without alcohol. As with all of these alcohol-free white and rosé wines, make sure you serve this really well chilled if you want it to taste as wine-like as possible. It'll also dial down the sweetness a touch, as these wines do tend to be on the sweeter-than-normal side to make up for the lack of alcohol. I'd even chuck a few ice cubes in the glass with this one. I know, what a rebel!

TORRES NATUREO SYRAH DE-ALCOHOLISED WINE
0.5 PER CENT, £5.99 WIDELY AVAILABLE

Another one from Torres, this is their red take on non-alcoholic wine. And they've plumped for Syrah as their grape of choice. A wise choice, because this is a grape with lots of weight, colour and flavour once it's made into wine. The trick is then removing the alcohol without removing too much else. In which case, it worked. This has got lots of bright plum and black cherry fruit aromas and flavour, along with a lovely deep red colour. OK, so even on the nose you know it's not proper wine because it's a little light. And on the palate it has the fruit but not the weight that a similar wine with alcohol would have. But we've gone alcohol-free and this is pretty much as good as it's going to get if you want to drink wine without alcohol. Food friendly, too.

LUCKY SAINT UNFILTERED LAGER 330ML
0.5 PER CENT, £1.80 WIDELY AVAILABLE

Founder Luke Boase was so dedicated to the cause of creating a great-tasting alcohol-free beer that he gave his job (and drinking, come to think of it) to do it. Which is good news indeed because the results are jaw-droppingly good. The beer is unfiltered so retains as much flavour as possible, meaning you don't really miss the alcohol.

BREWDOG NANNY STATE 4 X 330ML
0.5 PER CENT, AROUND £4 WIDELY AVAILABLE
www.brewdog.com

One of the first and still one of the best low-alcohol beers around. It helps that being a hoppy ale, there are a lot more flavours in the glass compared to lager, so you miss the alcohol (or lack of) less. The people behind Brewdog make their low-alcohol beer differently to most. Instead of making the beer and then removing the alcohol, they brew a 0.5 per cent beer from the ground up, using a huge variety of speciality malts. These malts add flavour and body but don't provide any fermentable sugars, so the yeast doesn't have anything to convert to alcohol (nature's greatest party trick, that – converting sugar into alcohol). It's then generously dry-hopped so is unashamedly hoppy in taste with plenty of citrusy, spicy, woody flavours. And in the glass, it's the colour of treacle. Have this on the table with a plate piled high with sausages and mash.

WAITROSE LOW ALCOHOL CIDER 500ML
<1 PER CENT, AROUND £1.30
www.waitrose.com

When it comes to comparing apples with apples, take out the alcohol and we're usually left with something more watery than apple-y. Not in this case: from a Herefordshire producer and made from bittersweet apples, this is as near as dammit. Full of fresh fruit aromas and smooth flavours, it does a great job of tasting like cider.

PART THREE

Ready to Drink

These are the drinks I reach for during the day, when water gets boring, when I want something with an instant kick of flavour. But there's no mixing needed, no pimping to be done; just open and pour into a glass. The choice of drinks in this category is quite amazing, thanks to a number of great producers getting creative with flavours without the use of artificial ones. With more producers springing up all the time, you will find everything from pressés to kombucha (made from fermented tea) in this category. What makes the drinks I've picked here stand out is the balance of flavour, freshness and the fact that they feel more grown-up than most other soft drinks on offer. And unlike some that contain more sugar than a can of Coke, these ones hit the not-too-sweet spot with refreshing accuracy. Plus, they're all easy to find on the shelves or online.

....

LUSCOMBE ORGANIC HOT GINGER BEER 27CL
AROUND £1.50 WIDELY AVAILABLE
www.luscombe.co.uk

This Devon drinks company makes a mouth-wateringly good selection of grown-up, fruit-based soft drinks and one of the best ginger beers around. This one's much drier and a whole lot more ginger-y in flavour than most, making it gorgeous enough to go alcohol-free, no problem. Made from ginger root and with a dash of Sicilian lemon, this is fiery, fresh and gently fizzy. The big flavours mean it can cope with plenty of hearty food flavours too, especially anything with spice.

URBAN CORDIAL APPLE, CINNAMON & CLOVE 500ML

AROUND £6

www.urbancordial.com

Created by founder Natasha Steele when she couldn't find anything non-alcoholic to drink, she started making cordials using fruit from her allotment and selling them at local farmers' markets. Before long she was sourcing surplus fruit from farms in Kent to make more, and to date she's saved more than 50 tonnes of fruit going to landfill.

There is a whole range of flavours, but this one is a particular favourite, and I usually just mix it with still or sparkling water, one part cordial to eight parts water. It's also lovely served warm in colder months. The entire range is low sugar with at least 50% less sugar and at least 50% more fruit than other brands and there are no artificial flavours or sweeteners in there, just natural ingredients and bags of flavour.

LUSCOMBE DAMASCENE ROSE BUBBLY 32CL
12 X 270ML, £21.30
www.luscombe.co.uk

The prettiest drink, this one's a blooming marvellous combination of spring water, organic grape juice and organic Damascene rosewater. But rather than tasting like perfume, there are notes of lemon and blueberry too, rounding out the flavours rather beautifully. With tiny, long-lasting bubbles and just a hint of pink to the colour, it looks gorgeous in the glass. Serve it in a flute for maximum sparkling effect.

MOTHER ROOT GINGER SWITCHEL 480ML
£19
www.motherroot.london

Founder Bethan Higson had the idea for Mother Root back when she was pregnant herself and was struggling to find interesting things to drink. Based on an old American 'shrub' recipe of apple cider vinegar, honey and ginger, she's added a touch of chilli, too. The idea is you add a small dash of it to a glass with ice and top up with soda water, tonic water or just plain still or sparkling water. If you've got them to hand, add a twist of lemon peel or a sprig of rosemary. It's so fresh with beautifully balanced flavours and because of its tang, feels a world away from the usual notion of a soft drink. Note each bottle contains 20 x 24ml serves and keeps in the fridge for months once opened.

FEVER-TREE AROMATIC TONIC WATER 500ML

AROUND £1.95 WIDELY AVAILABLE

www.fever-tree.com

Created as a mixer for Pink G&Ts (which is how I first drank it), I cracked open a bottle of this one dry evening and poured it into a heavy tumbler with nothing but a handful of ice. What a hit: a grown-up drink with a hint of bitterness, thanks to the combination of quinine in the tonic and the addition of angostura bark extract. Of course you could just add a few drops of Angostura bitters to your usual tonic but this one contains other botanicals, including cardamom and ginger, and the colour is just pink enough to make it look fabulous in the glass. Add a twist of lemon peel and it's just the tonic. Good value for money, too. On non-dry evenings, this is absolutely made for strong, juniper-heavy gins such as Plymouth Gin or Sipsmith's VJOP.

BELVOIR ELDERFLOWER PRESSÉ 750ML
AROUND £2.60 WIDELY AVAILABLE
www.belvoirfarm.co.uk

Packed with the heady, earthy scent of elderflowers, this really does smell hedgerow-fresh. Big on aroma and flavour but with pleasingly small and long-lasting bubbles, it's made with local spring water, fresh lemon juice and lots of fresh elderflowers. For the same price, you can go for the light option, with a touch less sugar. Personally I'd rather have a bit more sugar and a lot more balance and flavour.

BOTTLEGREEN CRISP APPLE SPARKLING PRESSE 750ML

AROUND £2.95 WIDELY AVAILABLE
www.bottlegreendrinks.com

Bottlegreen were among the first to take elderflower cordial into the mainstream. And given how much I drank of the stuff when pregnant, into my bloodstream. Their elderflower pressé is a little on the light side for me (I want pungent) but I love their apple take on the pressé, probably because it smells a little bit like cider. Whatever, it's lovely; the flavours are bright, balanced and fresh. There's sweetness, but not too much.

JUKES 6
9X30ML, £35 WIDELY AVAILABLE
www.jukescordialities.com

This is another switchel, basically flavoured apple cider vinegar with additional natural flavourings. But this one's created by wine expert Matthew Jukes and designed to be drunk in place of your usual glass of red, white or rosé wine. Of the three currently available, this is my pick of the bunch, a 'red' with warming blackberry fruits and a touch of spice. Mix a splash of the cordial with still water and treat them as you would wine – swirl, sniff, slurp – served in your smartest wine glasses. Great with food, too.

LA BREWERY TROPICAL GINGER KOMBUCHA 300ML
AROUND £2.95 OCADO

Made by the Suffolk-based non-alcoholic LA Brewery, this is
a bit like ginger ale but made from kombucha (think
fermented tea, nicer than it sounds I promise you) by
fermentation and foraging fanatic, Louise Avery. Naturally
low in sugar and packed with gut-friendly bacteria, it's made
with ginger, hops and the citrusy yuzu fruit. Fresh, lightly
fizzy and good for you to boot! Her whole range is a delight,
but another favourite is the Suffolk Blush, one of the best
alcohol-free pink fizzes I've tried.

PART FOUR

How to Be a Good Non-Drinker

It's all well and good going dry for a spell but it's not always easy being a non-drinker, especially if you're the only one in the room. But with a little know-how – and sometimes preparation – there are ways to make it easier. Here's a quick look at some of the most common scenarios, along with a few ideas on how to sail through them, glass of something alcohol-free in hand.

AT A PARTY

Assuming you are going to the party rather than throwing one, the first thing to do is make sure you take something non-alcoholic to drink with you. And whatever you take should be simple to help yourself to, so a bottle of something readymade (and ready-chilled if needs be) is best. If you know you are going to be surrounded by people drinking wine, take a non-alcoholic wine or something that looks wine-like and drink it out of a wine glass or flute. And keep yourself topped up so that you don't have to refuse a top-up from someone else. That way, no one will notice, you won't be asked why you're not drinking and it won't become a *thing*. Because the interesting thing about not drinking when you're at a party is other people's reactions: most will be fleetingly interested before moving on to talk about something else. But if someone sees it as a *Big Deal*, it's a little tedious.

Also, don't just take a bottle of something non-alcoholic or alcohol-free for yourself; take a bottle of wine for the party-giver too.

WHEN PREGNANT

As if the swollen ankles, hot flushes and constant loo trips weren't enough to put up with, you can't drink either. Latest government guidelines advise that no alcohol is consumed when pregnant. I was pregnant/breastfeeding for about five years on and off, but that was back when one or two glasses of wine per week weren't considered the work of the devil. Not that I felt like going anywhere near a glass of wine until at least after the halfway mark. I definitely enjoyed the odd small glass a couple of times a week but really, I preferred a cold glass of something gingery, which seemed to help ease nauseous waves. Or a cup of hot water with a chunk of ginger thrown in, or a cup of herbal tea (not raspberry leaf, though. As I said earlier I'm never going near that stuff again. Drank gallons to induce labour. Didn't work, ever).

Anything carbonated played havoc in the later stages of pregnancy so I stuck to non-fizzy drinks. A glass of cold water with ice, a squeeze of fresh lemon or lime, a sprinkling of salt flakes and a sprig of mint is a quick-fix favourite, pregnant or not. You could of course switch the salt for a pinch of sugar if you prefer, depending on what your taste buds are craving.

And we can't talk pregnancy without talking elderflower. According to folklore, elders have particularly relevant medicinal properties. Apparently the bark hastens labour and the berries soothe piles. Just as well, really. Anyway, we've already covered elderflower cordial (see pages 11–13) and pressé (see page 53) but if you want to avoid bubbles, stick with a small dash of cordial and mix it with cold, still water and lots of ice.

IN RESTAURANTS & PUBS

Increasingly, restaurants are taking non-alcoholic drinks very seriously indeed. And not just with a list of mocktails that are no more than watered-down fruit juice with lots of ice and a straw. Each year a growing number of dry bars and restaurants are opening. Redemption was one of the first to open in London back in 2013 with drinks on offer like the Beet-o-tini (homemade beetroot juice, freshly squeezed orange juice, lime and coconut water, shaken over ice) and the Coco-rita (coconut water, lime and agave syrup, shaken over ice and served in a salt-rimmed glass like a margarita). In Bristol, The Ethicurean (www.theethicurean.com) is famed for making their own drinks from foraged ingredients and creates food-friendly options to match what's on the menu. And last year saw the opening of the UK's first alcohol free off-licence just off Regent Street in London's West End. The times, they are a-changing.

In most pubs, though, a Lime & Soda is about the most exotic thing on offer. And fruit juice doesn't count as a grown-up drink. In which case, I'll ask for a small bottle of tonic water with a slice of lime and lots of ice.

WHEN YOU'RE TRAINING

Now, I'm not going to pretend I have ever trained for anything other than my wine exams but if you're training for something that requires your body to do amazing things, like run a 5K or even a marathon, then there are a couple of things to bear in mind about alcohol. Crucially, it's a powerful diuretic, meaning it makes you wee more and so dehydrates the body. This will have a negative impact on your sleep, as well as lowering blood sugar levels – both things you need to bank if you're expecting your body to do great things. A glass of wine the night before running the parents' race at school isn't exactly going to ruin your chances but if you're aiming for something rather more substantial, alcohol is going to hinder rather than help your body prepare.

AT HOME

On my dry days, there are certain triggers I avoid so as not to lead to temptation. The biggest one for me is nuts, as in actual big salted peanuts. If I so much as go near a peanut at around 7 p.m., I'll want a cold glass of wine to go with it. But take away the nuts and I won't think about it. Another trigger point is when my husband comes back from work and pours himself a beer. If I'm having a dry day, I'll make sure I've already got something delicious and alcohol-free on the go.

And now, just as I would pick a bottle of wine, I'll pick a different non-alcoholic drink each week, whether it's a bottle of ginger beer or tonic water, tomato juice or an alcohol-free bottle of beer so that there's always something to choose from. I do at least two dry days a week – it's the only 5:2 you'll find me doing – and I usually mix it up from week to week so that it feels less like a routine, picking my dry days in advance. It doesn't always work but for the most part it definitely makes life easier, not to mention slightly healthier.

PART FIVE

What to Drink When You're Drinking

One of my favourite pastimes during dry spells is planning which wines I'll be enjoying a glass of with dinner/friends once the dry spell is up. I know, not entirely normal, but we really are spoilt for choice. Here are some of the current movers and shakers to look out for when topping up the wine rack.

....

COOL COUNTRIES

As much as I love a big old glass of robust red filled with fruit flavours, if I'm going to have a couple of glasses of something I'd rather it was on the lighter side; in weight, flavour and alcohol. And the best place to find those wines is from a cool-climate wine region. To understand why this makes a difference, we need to take a quick look at how climate affects a grape. Simply put, the more sun a grape gets, the riper it will be. And the riper it is, the more sugar it'll have in it. Given that winemaking is about converting the sugar in grapes into alcohol, the riper a grape is at the start, the more alcohol it'll have by the time it's in your glass. So, grapes grown in warm regions generally make more weighty wines than those grown in cool regions.

The hallmark of cool-climate wines is naturally lower alcohol levels, along with a typically lighter, fresher build than wines from warm regions. Obviously, latitude plays a large part but you'll find these cooler regions in most wine-producing countries, tucked away in places either near the coast or up in the foothills of mountain ranges. And the best wines come from grapes that love being in a cool climate, because it doesn't suit every grape. Just as I know I'm not made for wearing jumpsuits (I look like a giant toddler if you *must* know!), some grapes just can't style out too little sun. Natural cool-climate grapes include Chardonnay, Pinot Noir, Riesling and a load of amazing, unusual ones found off the beaten track. Here are some of the coolest wines to look out for.

English Sparkling Wine

It's been a long time coming but finally, *finally*, English wine is A Thing. England is pretty cool temperature-wise compared with most wine-producing regions. But thanks to the temperature warming up by a few degrees (possibly global warming's only upside) and with the right grapes planted in the right places, things have changed dramatically over the last twenty years. By planting the classic Champagne grapes – Chardonnay, Pinot Noir and Pinot Meunier – on chalky soils, England now produces some of the best traditional method (meaning they're made in the same way as Champagne) sparkling wines in the world. They're typically crisp, with pure fruit flavours. Even one of the most famous names in Champagne, Taittinger, has bought a vineyard in Kent. Names to look out for include Wiston, The Grange, Black Chalk, Gusbourne and Breaky Bottom.

And although most of what's produced across England and Wales is sparkling, there are some gorgeous wines being made there, without bubbles. It's the cool-climate-loving grapes that are making the most interesting wines; one of my favourites is an orchard-scented white made from the Bacchus grape by Albourne Estate in Sussex. And watch out for English Pinot Noir – they're getting better with every (good) vintage.

Cool Là Là!

France has got plenty of cool spots, the most famous being Champagne. It's tough to get grapes to ripen when they're planted so far from the equator, but when it comes to making Champagne that's just what's needed. Because to make great Champagne, you need grapes with plenty of acidity so that by the time they've been made into wine and knocked about some more while undergoing a second fermentation in the bottle, they can still produce something crisp and fresh.

But another rather more underrated, relatively cool-climate region is the Loire Valley. What I really love about the wines from this region is their freshness. The whites produced at either end of the Loire – Muscadet at the western end, Sancerre and Pouilly Fumé at the eastern end – are brilliantly bright and expressive. And the reds made from the Cabernet Franc grape are blatantly fragrant. Again, it's the naturally higher acidity in these wines that gives them such a fresh edge.

And then there's the Jura region, tucked away in eastern France. Like its nearest neighbouring wine region, Burgundy, you'll find Chardonnay and Pinot Noir here. But there's also a treasure trove of brilliantly original grapes that are made into brilliantly original wines. The region is famous for its Vin Jaune (yellow wine), made from the Savagnin grape and left to age for years in old oak barrels. With their intense nutty flavours, these sherry-like wines are quite something, if you like that sort of thing. But there are plenty of crisp, dry whites made from the Savagnin grape too, often blended with Chardonnay, that give you a taste of the Jura without having to go completely yellow. As for the reds, try one made from the Trousseau grape if you can find one. It's a bit like Pinot Noir can be – light and spicy – but not quite as polished (in a good way). Cool hunting!

German Riesling

Some of Germany's vineyards are even further north than Champagne and so steep they're a nightmare to harvest. But there's a particular grape that makes it all worthwhile – Riesling. Wine nerds go particularly nuts over this grape (which they'll pronounce 'reese-ling', by the way) because it manages to produce wines from here with an incredible balance of freshness and sweetness that you won't find anywhere else. And the style of wines made by this one grape from south-facing slate-covered slopes along the Mosel and Rhine rivers ranges from Aga-top dry to almost indecently sweet. German wine labels are sometimes a more difficult read than Kafka, but if you want something lip-smackingly crisp, with pure citrus flavours and refreshingly lower alcohol (usually around 9 per cent), look out for the word *trocken*, meaning 'dry'.

For reds, get your lips around Spätburgunder. You already know this grape, just under another name. It's Pinot Noir and in Germany it produces gorgeous, light, red fruit-filled reds with an underlying earthiness, particularly from the cool Ahr region.

Brave (Cool) New World

It's not just Old World wines that have the cool factor. There are plenty of vineyard sites in New World countries like South Africa, Chile and Australia that can be described as cool climate when it comes to making wine. In South Africa, pockets of vineyards close to the coast and to the west of the Cape benefit from bracing Atlantic sea breezes that help slow down the grape ripening process. (As with cooking, blast it and the flavours burn off, but cook it slow and low and the flavours intensify.) Look out for brisk whites from the Darling River, Elgin or Elim regions, especially Sauvignon Blanc. For reds, try Pinot Noir from the Walker Bay region, especially from vineyards near the coastal town of Hermanus.

In Australia, it's not all blazing sun and cork hats. Some of the best wine regions have distinctly cool parts to them, including the Yarra Valley in Victoria, where Pinot Noir and Chardonnay are particularly at home. For great Riesling, head to Western Australia's Great Southern region and South Australia's Eden Valley, where a bit of elevation goes a long way. And for cool-climate Chardonnay, Pinot Noir and even Shiraz, there are plenty of devilishly good wines made in Tasmania.

New Zealand's Marlborough region and Sauvignon Blanc are made for each other, thanks to a cool maritime climate and plenty of sunshine hours allowing the grapes to ripen slowly. That's what gives the grapes their signature cool-climate acidity, translating as freshness in the wines. Further south on New Zealand's South Island, Central Otago is the world's most southerly wine region. In summer, the days are hot but the nights are cool, again slowing down ripening times for the grapes. Unsurprisingly, some of the best wines here are made from the Pinot Noir grape. Aromatic whites are also worth foraging for, including Riesling and Pinot Gris (think Pinot Grigio but with more interesting flavours).

In Chile, new cooler-than-your-average regions have been popping up recently, thanks to the double whammy of the Pacific Ocean down one side of the country and the Andes Mountains on the other. The romantically named Casablanca Valley was the original cool region, known for its fabulously fresh Sauvignon Blanc wines. Now, look out for wines from the ocean-influenced Leyda Valley too, great for Sauvignon Blanc, Pinot Noir and Chardonnay.

IS THERE ANY SUCH THING AS 'HEALTHY' WINE?

We know that alcohol kills germs dead but still you can't really call wine 'healthy' – mainly because it's got alcohol in it and too much alcohol is definitely not good for us. (Current government recommended limits are now just fourteen units a week for both men and women, or seven to ten glasses of wine a week depending on the size of the glass and the strength of what's in it.) But there are lots of wines around that claim to be somewhat more *virtuous* than others. I'm talking about the organic ones, the biodynamic ones, the natural ones, the low-sulphur ones and the low-sugar ones. So what do all these different wine categories mean? And are they any good? Let's start by getting the skinny on skinny.

Skinny Wines

Rather inconveniently, alcohol is fattening. It's more calorie-laden than sugar, in fact. So, a wine that's high in alcohol and sugar (whether that sugar is natural or added) is going to contain more calories than one with relatively low alcohol and little or no sugar. A glass of wine will vary in calorie content depending on the wine and the size of the glass but, on average, a standard 175ml glass of dry red or white wine can be anything between 120–160 calories. Anything with lashings of alcohol and/or more sugar will be more.

And just to top it off, alcohol contains almost the same calories per gram as fat, but unlike fat there's no such thing as good or bad alcohol; rather, alcohol has no nutritional value at all. They're completely 'empty' calories *sad face*.

The good news is that if you're cutting down on sugar, wine isn't *that* bad if you stick to the dry stuff. A standard glass of dry red or white wine contains the equivalent to less than half a teaspoon of sugar and (in most cases) comes from the fruit sugars in grapes rather than added sugar. A glass of Prosecco contains the equivalent of around a teaspoon of sugar, which is why it's just so damn quaffable.

Talking of bubbles, there are plenty of low- or no-sugar sparkling options to choose from. For Champagne, look for the words 'Brut Nature' or 'Extra Brut' on the label. This tells you that little or no sugar (known as dosage) is added at the end of the fermentation process. This isn't a new fad; one particular Champagne house was making it as far back as the late nineteenth century. If you don't want to spend Champagne money, seek out a Brut Nature-labelled Cava instead (it's made in the same way as Champagne), but do prepare the taste buds: these wines are searingly dry.

There are a few Prosecco and Champagne brands that market themselves as having lower sugar at around 70 calories per small glass (both would normally be around 100 calories for a small glass). Thing is, there's still alcohol in there and that's the really fattening part. The best option is to go for something that's naturally low in alcohol and sugar. And there are plenty of those to choose from *happy face*.

Because the level of alcohol is determined by the sugar levels in the grape at the point when they're picked (see, you already knew that), cooler regions are more likely to produce wines with naturally lower sugar levels than those made from super-ripe grapes from warmer wine regions. Muscadet wines are typically dry at around 11–12 per cent alcohol. So, a small glass (125ml, the same size as a Champagne flute – I'm doing small glasses because you wanted skinny) has around 80 calories. Riesling, especially from Germany, is usually between 9 and 11 per cent alcohol. Again, a 125ml glass will be around 70–90 calories depending on the exact alcohol content. The same goes for a glass of Vinho Verde, a naturally lower-alcohol dry white wine from northern Portugal, usually around 9–11 per cent alcohol. And there's a northern Spanish white called Txakoli (pronounced 'cha-koh-lee') that's usually around 10 per cent. The first sip will see you sucking your cheeks in (that's the acidity) but after that, it is fabulous. One particular producer in New Zealand has made a Marlborough Sauvignon Blanc at just 9.5 per cent alcohol (compared to the more usual 12–13 per cent for New Zealand Sauvignon Blanc). Made by Forrest, their Doctor's Sauvignon Blanc (£8.99, widely available) is made with a little extra bit of technical know-how in order to reduce the alcohol and a small glass is around 100 calories. Well worth making an appointment to try it.

Of course you could just have a glass of whatever you fancy, but make it a half glass – and definitely no peanuts.

Organic Wines

I've lost count of the times that people have asked me if it's true that organic wines are less likely to give them a headache. Before we look at that, let's establish what makes a wine organic in the first place. Basically it means that the wine must be made from organically grown grapes. No pesticides, fertilisers or fungicides are used in the vineyards. Which is obviously a Good Thing. But that doesn't necessarily mean they won't have any additives like sulphur in them, although most organic wines do have less than your average bottle.

The reason why sulphur is used when making wine in the first place is it helps keep air away from the unfermented grape juice and the resulting wine, so the liquid in question doesn't oxidise and spoil. Think what happens when you take a bite of an apple and leave it on the side for a few moments (or in the case of my children, the entire apple core. Drives me nuts!). Anyway, by the time you go back to it, the flesh has started to turn brown. This is because oxygen has got to it and the flesh has oxidised. Wine that's oxidised loses flavour, structure and general loveliness. Sulphur is a barrier to oxygen and acts as a disinfectant, helping to minimise any undesirable aromas and flavours created by yeast beasts and bacteria.

Anyway, there are limits to how much sulphur is allowed in wine and most producers use well below that amount. And interestingly, lots of food and drink products – dried fruit, ketchup, fruit juice, to name a few – have far higher levels of sulphur in them. There are some unlucky folk who are allergic to sulphur but for most of us, it's not the sulphur causing the headache. It's more likely the amount we've drunk, along with lack of water and/or food, unfortunately.

Biodynamic Wines

These wines are in a kind of holistic super-organic category of their own. Made according to three basic principles, first and foremost the vineyard that produces biodynamic wines must be sustainable. It will be treated throughout the growing cycle with herb- and mineral-based 'preparations' (including powdered cow horn). And techniques like pruning, picking and bottling are done according to lunar, solar, planetary and stellar rhythms. The wines won't be fined or filtered as most wines are (a process to take any lumps and bumps out of the wine before it's bottled) and the use of sulphur is minimal, if added at all. It might sound kooky to some but the proof is in the pudding. Or rather, in the glass – some of the world's most famous (and expensive) wine producers make their wines biodynamically and they are spectacular. One thing: they don't come cheap. Making wine like this costs money. But as supporters of biodynamic wines will tell you, they don't cost the earth. Literally.

Natural Wines

Here's another wine trend that's gone a bit bonkers over the last few years. Started by a group of small-scale wine producers, mainly in France and Italy but now found all over the world, natural wines are made with little or no intervention either in the vineyard or in the winery. They're made from organic or biodynamically grown grapes, with no additives used (although some will have a little bit of sulphur added before bottling). As yet, there's still no official classification for natural wines. And the level of 'naturalness' can vary from one natural winemaker to the next so it's hard to generalise about how they taste. The best way I can describe the ones I've tried and loved is that they have a real vibrancy about them, along with a kind of earthiness. I've also had ones that tasted more like cider than wine – not so enjoyable, to be honest. But that's the point: these wines are a little more out there in style.

It's not always easy to spot a natural wine on the shelf, because it won't necessarily tell you that it's a natural wine on the label. Rather, you have to know which producers make natural wines. But there are plenty of specialist wine shops with natural wines on their shelves, along with online wine retailers that can point you in the right (virtual) direction. Try Buon Vino (buonvino.co.uk) and Les Caves de Pyrene (lescaves.co.uk) for some natural wine inspiration.

Orange Wines

These might be all the rage but actually, they've been around for centuries in places like Georgia, Slovenia and Italy. Basically, they're wines made from white grapes but – as with red wines – the juice is left in contact with the skins while it ferments. The resulting colour is more orange than yellow and the exact shade of colour will depend on the length of skin contact. Sometimes known as amber wines rather than orange, they're distinctly tannic compared with more conventionally made white wines. And the flavours are more intense, many with a kind of nuttiness to them. With little or no added sulphur, these are good wines to seek out if you want to keep things natural. But they are fairly hard to find – and you've got to like your wines on the dry, tannic side. In my experience, they're best served slightly chilled (not too much or the tannins will take over) and with a huge plate of cold meats in front of you to show off the flavours of the wine in a flattering light.

ONE LAST DROP . . .

So now that you have a stash of grown-up, booze-free drinks at your disposal, go forth and fill your dry days (or rather, evenings) with flavour. Have a glass of something that tastes like wine, beer or even a G&T and pimp your sparkling water like never before. Whether it's for a couple of days a week, a week every month or a month every year, I hope that I've given you some divine drinks inspiration. And just as important (to me, anyway), that you are full of ideas for the wines that you're going to enjoy when you're not dry.

As I told you at the start, I never, ever thought I'd be writing a book about *not* drinking. But as much as I love my wine, I know that dry days are good for my health. And best of all, it makes me really appreciate what I do drink on my non-dry days. Here's to making the most of whatever's in our glass!

Acknowledgements

Enormous thanks to all the people who've made this updated edition possible including Sarah Thomas and Ben McConnell at Little, Brown and my agent Heather Holden-Brown and all the team at HHB. Thank you to all my readers of the Knackered Mother's Wine Club. I appreciate every single one of your comments and love hearing from you, *raises glass* you are amazing! Finally, to my family, for still letting me think I'm really interesting when I talk about wine. I love you all.

Further Reference

THE KNACKERED MOTHER'S WINE CLUB

twitter: @knackeredmutha
instagram: @knackeredmother
www.knackeredmotherswineclub.com

BOOKS

Craddock, Harry, *The Savoy Cocktail Book* (Girard & Stewart, 2015).

McDonald, Claire and Lucy, *The Crumbs Family Cookbook: 150 Really Quick and Very Easy Recipes* (CICO Books, 2014).

McGinn, Helen, *The Knackered Mother's Wine Club: Everything You Need to Know About Wine – and Much, Much More* (Pan, 2014).

WEBSITES

www.alcoholfree.co.uk (The Alcohol-Free Shop)

www.badoit.com

www.brewdog.com

www.buonvino.co.uk

www.fever-tree.com

www.cipriani.com/us/harrys-bar

www.healthydoc.com (Dr Nigma Talib)

www.lakeland.co.uk

www.lescaves.co.uk

www.luscombe.co.uk

www.marksandspencer.com

www.pomegreat.com

www.sainsburys.co.uk

www.schweppes.com

www.seedlipdrinks.com

www.teisseire.com/en-gb/uk

www.theethicurean.com

www.thetomatostall.co.uk

www.waitrose.com

Index

diuretics 62
'dry' restaurants/bars 61

Eisberg Alcohol-Free Rosé 42
Eisberg Alcohol-Free
    Sauvignon Blanc NV 40
elderberry 60
elderflower 69–70
    Belvoir Elderflower Pressé
        53
    Elderflower Fizz 11
    Homemade Elderflower
        Cordial 12–13
equipment xvi
espresso, Coffee Tonic 10

Fellini 20–1
Fever-Tree Aromatic Tonic
    Water 52
Fizzero 38
Forrest's Doctor's Sauvignon
    Blanc 74
French wines 68–9

German wines 36, 69–70, 74
gin xi, xii, xviii, 4, 52
gin substitutes *see* Seedlip &
    Tonic
ginger
    Spiced Chai Latte 31–2
    Warm Apple Punch 29–30
ginger ale
    Ginger & Basil Sparkler 3
    Luscombe Organic Hot
        Ginger Beer 48
    Mosc-No Mule 17
    Shirley 24
glasses xvi

grape juice, Luscombe
    Damascene Rose Bubbly
        50
grapefruit, Light Sea Breeze
    23
grenadine xvii
    Pink Lemonade 14
    Shirley 24

'healthy' wines xiii, 72–8
    biodynamic wines 76, 77
    natural wines 77
    orange wines 78
    organic wines 75–6
    skinny wines 72–5
Hermanus 70

ice xviii

Jukes 6 55
Jura region 68, 69

La Brewery Tropical Ginger
    Beer 56
La Gioisa 35
lemon
    Almost 75 22
    Cos-No 25
    Pink Lemonade 14
lemonade
    Fellini 20–1
    Pink Lemonade 14
Les Caves de Pyrene 77
Light Sea Breeze 23
lime
    Cos-No 25
    Fresh Lime Soda 26
    No-Jito 18–19